Count Down to Fall

By Fran Hawk

Illustrated by Sherry Neidigh

Ten sweet gum leaves,
orange, purple, and red,
look like bright colored stars
as they fall on earth's bed.

Nine dogwood leaves
bright shining scarlet,
drifting down, down, down—
like the tail of a comet.

Eight beech tree leaves,
like yellow cats' eyes
float gently down
through autumn skies.

Seven pine cones,
and needles too,
pile on the ground
for squirrels to chew.

Six linden leaves
in Valentine shapes
reflect golden sun
in autumn's landscape.

Five prickly cases
with nuts, brown and hard,
pull leaves along with them
as they thump in the yard.

Four craggy oak leaves,
yellow, gold, and brown,
tumble with the acorns
that wear rough, shaggy crowns.

Three-pointed maple leaves,
yellow, orange, and red,
bring "helicopters" with them
as they twirl and spin ahead.

Oval, yellow birch leaves
drop two, by two, by two.
Natives used birch bark
to build their canoes.

One quaking aspen leaf,
yellow as butter,
twists in the breeze.
as it shimmers and flutters.

Needles and nuts
and pods and seeds
collect on the ground
with the cones and the leaves.

For Creative Minds

Plant Parts

Match the plant part to the picture. Answers are upside down at the bottom of the page.

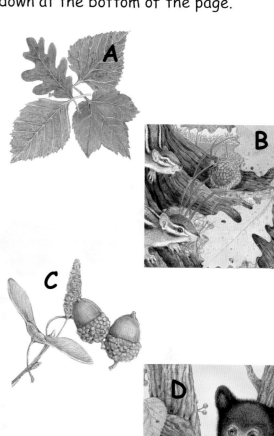

1 Think of stems (trunks are a type of stem) as "pipes" or "straws" to carry the water and nutrients from the roots to the leaves. They are also a type of support to keep the plant standing up so that the leaves can reach sunlight.

2 Seeds to help new plants grow are found in plant flowers, fruit, or nuts (including pinecones). The seeds need to be carried away from the parent plant so that they have enough room, nutrients, and sunlight to grow.

3 Roots are usually not visible since they are typically underground. Not only do they keep the plant in one place, but they absorb water and nutrients out of the ground for the plant to grow.

4 The green color in leaves comes from chlorophyll. When the days start to get shorter and cooler in the fall, many leaves stop making food and the chlorophyll (green color) goes away. Some of the colors that are left have been there all year long but the green covers them up! Trees survive the winter on food they have stored in their roots.

5 The leaves make food for the plant to grow. They use chlorophyll reacting in sunlight to take the water and nutrients that were absorbed by the roots and carried up by the stem and combine it with gas (carbon dioxide) that they absorb from the air. This makes a type of sugar (glucose) that gives the plants the energy they need to grow and give off the oxygen that we need to breathe. This is called photosynthesis.

Answers: 1D, 2C, 3B, 4A, 5E

Leaves—The Shape of it All

Leaves come in all shapes and sizes. In the fall, as the weather gets colder, they come in all different colors, too! Leaf shapes include round, oval, diamond-shaped, triangular, long and narrow, fan-shaped, or even mitten-shaped. Some leaves have smooth edges, some have toothed edges, and some are lobed. Match the leaf to its type (answers are upside-down at the bottom of the page):

smooth edges   toothed edges   lobed   needled

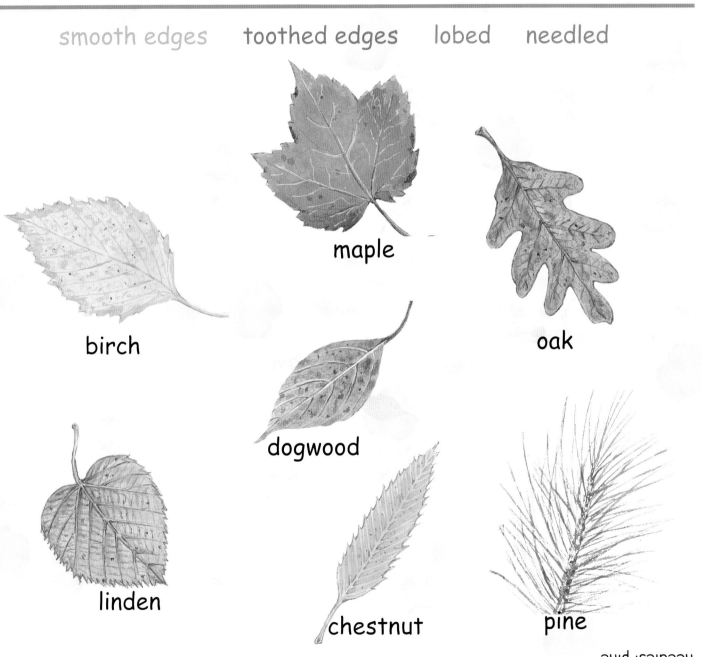

birch

maple

oak

dogwood

linden

chestnut

pine

What Good Are Plants?

Plants are producers and are near the bottom of the food chain. Every animal depends on plants to survive – even if the animal doesn't eat the plants themselves! All kinds of animals eat plants. We eat lots of things that come from plants. What are some things that you eat from plants?

Plants give us the oxygen that we need to breathe.

Some animals build their shelter in or around plants; or they might use plant material to build their nests.

Animals might hide in or around plants to protect themselves from predators or to wait for prey.

Here are just a few ways that people or animals use some of the trees mentioned in the book.

Maple
We eat the syrup on pancakes.
Deer and moose eat the bark.

Birch
Deer eat the leaves.
Native Americans used the bark for their canoes.

Pine
Squirrels and other animals eat the seeds in pinecones. We use the wood for building houses and furniture.

Quaking Aspen
Deer and elk love eating the leaves. Beavers eat aspen, as well as use it for building their homes.

Oaks
Squirrels and chipmunks eat the acorns.
Deer eat all parts of the tree. We use wood for furniture and floors.

Match the Leaves

Using the information and the illustrations in the book, match the fall leaves to the summer leaves. Answers are upside down at the bottom of the page.

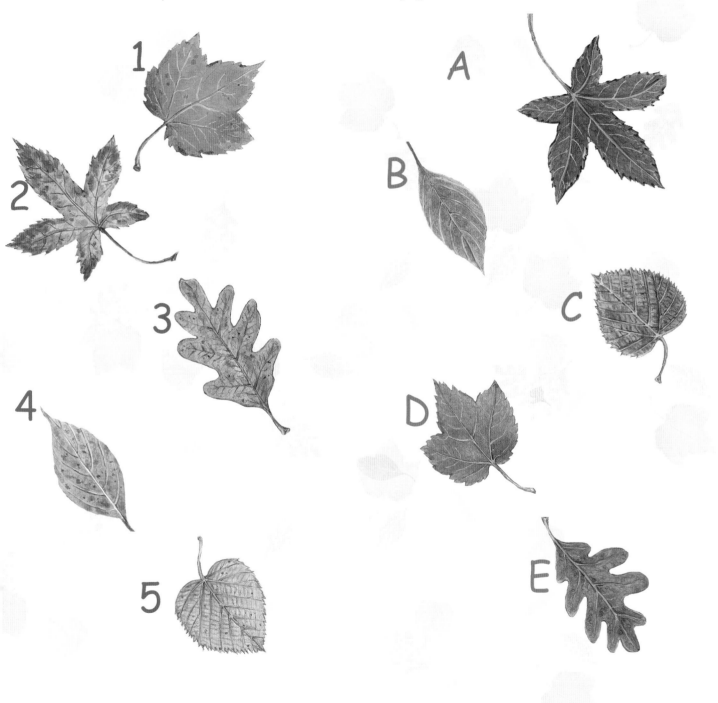

Thanks to Dr. John O'Keefe and Pamela M. Snow at Fisher Museum, Harvard Forest and to Robert Smith, Arborist, and Susan Erickson, Research Coordinator, of the Arbor Day Foundation for verifying the accuracy of the information in this book.

Publisher's Cataloging-In-Publication Data

Hawk, Fran.
  Count down to fall / by Fran Hawk ; illustrated by Sherry Neidigh.
    p. : col. ill. ; cm.
  Summary: Count backwards from ten to one during one of the most colorful times of the year. Learn about the bright, colorful leaves and the trees from which they fall. Watch the animals frolicking in the crisp, autumn air as they get ready for the approaching cold winter. Includes section "For Creative Minds" with activities.
    Interest age level: 004-008.
    Interest grade level: P-3.
    ISBN: 978-1-934359-94-5 (hardcover)
    ISBN: 978-1-607180-39-5 (pbk.)
    ISBN: 978-1-607180-59-3 (English eBook)
    ISBN: 978-1-607180-49-4 (Spanish eBook)
  1. Autumn--Juvenile literature. 2. Fall foliage--Juvenile literature. 3. Animals--Habits and behavior--Juvenile literature. 4. Trees--Juvenile literature. 5. Autumn. 6. Animals--Habits and behavior. 7. Trees. I. Neidigh, Sherry. II. Title. Title.

QB637.7 .H29 2009
508.2   2009922605

Lexile Level: 1070, Lexile Code: AD

Manufactured in China, January 2010
This product conforms to CPSIA 2008
2 3 4 5 6 7 8 9 10 11

Sylvan Dell Publishing
976 Houston Northcutt Blvd., Suite 3
Mt. Pleasant, SC 29464